W9-AOY-161

	DATE DUE		

RECORD BREAKERS

BREAKERS

The Living World

For a free color catalog describing Gareth Stevens Publishing's list of high-quality books and multimedia programs, call 1-800-542-2595 (USA) or 1-800-461-9120 (Canada). Gareth Stevens Publishing's Fax: (414) 225-0377. See our catalog, too, on the World Wide Web: http://gsinc.com

Library of Congress Cataloging-in-Publication Data

Lambert, David, 1932-
    The living world / written by David Lambert.
      p. cm. -- (Record breakers)
    Includes index.
    Summary: Provides information such as the tallest animals that ever lived, the largest insects, and the fastest animals.
    ISBN 0-8368-1949-7 (lib. bdg.)
    1. Natural history--Miscellanea--Juvenile literature.
    [1. Animals--Miscellanea.] I. Title. II. Series.
    QH48.L24   1997
    570--dc21   97-1126

First published in North America in 1997 by
Gareth Stevens Publishing
1555 North RiverCenter Drive, Suite 201
Milwaukee, Wisconsin 53212 USA

First published in 1994 by Watts Books, 96 Leonard Street, London, England, EC2A 4RH. Original © 1994 Orpheus Books Ltd. Illustrations by Mike Atkinson *(Garden Studio)*, Janos Marffy, David Wright *(Kathy Jakeman Illustration)*, Shane Marsh, David More *(Linden Artists)*, Betti Ferrero *(Milan Illustration Agency)*, Tim Hayward *(Bernard Thornton Artists)*, John Morris *(Wildlife Art Agency)*, and Steven Kirk. Created and produced by Nicholas Harris and Joanna Turner, Orpheus Books Ltd. Additional end matter © 1997 Gareth Stevens, Inc.

Printed in the United States of America

1 2 3 4 5 6 7 8 9 01 00 99 98 97

RECORD BREAKERS
The
Living World

by David Lambert

Gareth Stevens Publishing
MILWAUKEE

CONTENTS

Words that appear in the glossary are in **boldface** type the first time they occur in the text.

INTRODUCTION

AT LEAST 275,000 KINDS OF FLOWERING PLANTS exist today. There may be as many as 10 million kinds of animals. Thousands, perhaps millions more, died out long ago. Among these incredible numbers, a few plants and animals stand out from the rest because they are, or were, the largest, the smallest, or very special in some other way. Have you ever wondered — if you could hold a competition among all living things — which ones would win the top prizes?

In this book, you will discover that the heaviest whale, the blue whale, can weigh as much as 1,800 people. Yet, it would take more than a dozen of these whales to outweigh a giant sequoia tree, the heaviest living thing on Earth. Also, in this book, you will come across a living tree older than the pyramids of Egypt, and a mammal that can dive almost 2 miles (3 kilometers) beneath the surface of the ocean.

You'll read about the largest and smallest dinosaurs, the biggest-ever land mammals, the tallest animals that ever lived, and the tallest and shortest peoples. Here, too, are the speediest creatures on Earth, the animals that make the longest journeys around the world, and those that live the longest lives.

Welcome to the record breakers of the living world!

Arandaspis (above), one of the first-known fish, lived 480 million years ago. It had no fins and could not shut its mouth.

Eusthenopteron (above) was one of the first fish to breathe with lungs and use fins as "legs" to help it move around.

The small reptile Euparkeria (right) might have been the first animal to walk on two feet. It lived in southern Africa 240 million years ago.

Hylonomus (above) had waterproof skin and waterproof eggs. This small reptile, one of the earliest known, lived 320 million years ago in Canada.

Eoraptor (right) was one of the first dinosaurs. It was a two-legged, flesh-eating animal no bigger than a large dog. Eoraptor hunted small reptiles. It lived 228 million years ago in Argentina.

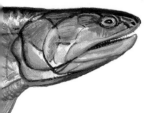

THE EARLIEST ANIMALS
FIRST OF THEIR KIND

ALL ANIMALS have prehistoric **ancestors** whose **fossil** remains are found in ancient rocks. Scientists studying these fossils can determine when each living group of animals appeared. Over the thousands of millions of years since life began, fossil history tells us that animals have — very gradually — changed. For example, various animals have grown a fin or a tail, developed wings, or lost teeth over time. This process is called **evolution.** When a new kind of animal evolves, an older one may die out, or become **extinct**. Jellyfish-like creatures, among the very earliest animals, appeared about 600 million years ago. Fifty million years later, the seas teemed with shellfish, worms, and animals with jointed legs. Later still, eel-like beasts with bony teeth appeared. These were probably the ancestors of fish, the earliest-known backboned animals. By about 400 million years ago, fish with lungs and fleshy fins began to move around on land. Forty million years later, these animals evolved into the first four-legged, backboned creatures — the **amphibians**. These animals could live on land, but they returned to the water to lay their eggs. It took another 80 million years for the first backboned animals to evolve — to live and breed on land. These were the first **reptiles**.

Illustrations are not drawn to scale.

Ichthyostega *(right)* was one of the earliest four-legged animals. This amphibian crawled through warm, swampy forests that existed in Greenland about 360 million years ago.

One of the earliest-known birds was Archaeopteryx. This crow-sized creature had feathered wings and was probably able to fly. But its teeth, claws, and bony tail were like those of a small, flesh-eating dinosaur. Archaeopteryx lived in Germany about 150 million years ago.

THE FIRST MAMMAL

Mammals are animals whose females produce milk to feed their young. The earliest-known mammals were tiny shrew-like creatures such as Megazostrodon and Kuehneotherium. They lived 220 million years ago in the shadows of the early dinosaurs, probably hunting for insects by night. Megazostrodon lived in southern Africa. Its relative Kuehneotherium lived in Britain.

THE LARGEST DINOSAURS
LARGEST-EVER LAND ANIMALS

M OST DINOSAURS are known only from a few bones, so scientists have had to estimate just how big these creatures were. As for the question of which was the biggest, the answer depends on whether the measurement is in height, length, or weight. The only fact upon which everyone agrees is that dinosaurs were the largest land animals that ever lived.

The heaviest and tallest dinosaur known from a complete skeleton was Brachiosaurus ("arm lizard"). A plump Brachiosaurus might have weighed more than 44 tons (40 metric tons) or as much as eight African elephants.

Mamenchisaurus ("Mamen Brook lizard") had the longest neck of all the dinosaurs. The longest dinosaur of all was Seismosaurus ("earth-shaking lizard"), perhaps longer than two tennis courts placed end to end. With its snaky neck, whiplike tail, and hollowed-out spinal bones, Seismosaurus was probably lighter than some of the shorter dinosaurs.

All these dinosaurs were plant-eaters. The meat-eaters, which needed to be quicker on their feet, were smaller. Even so, the largest of the meat-eaters, Tyrannosaurus rex ("king of the tyrant lizards") grew as heavy as an elephant.

PARADE OF THE GIANTS
If all the reptile record holders were gathered together, this *(below)* is how they would compare in size. All those shown — **pterosaurs**, crocodiles, and dinosaurs — belonged to the same group called archosaurs ("ruling reptiles").

Quetzalcoatlus ("feathered serpent") was a winged flying reptile, or pterosaur.

QUETZALCOATLUS
Wingspan: 39 feet (12 meters)
Largest-ever flying creature

Illustrations are approximately to scale.

TYRANNOSAURUS REX
39 feet (12 m) long
Up to 7.7 tons (7 metric tons)
Largest-ever land carnivore

DEINOSUCHUS
49 feet (15 m) long
Longest-known crocodile

Tyrannosaurus rex had jaws so huge that, if it were alive today, it could swallow people whole.

MAMENCHISAURUS
Neck 50 feet (15 m) long
Longest-necked animal

DIPLODOCUS
90 feet (27 m) long
*Longest dinosaur known
from complete skeleton*

SEISMOSAURUS
128-170 feet (39-52 m) long
Longest-ever dinosaur

STEGOSAURUS
30 feet (9 m) long
Largest plated dinosaur

Deinosuchus ("terrible crocodile") was a crocodile more than twice as long as the largest type of crocodile alive today.

BRACHIOSAURUS
72 feet (22 m) long
46 feet (14 m) tall
*Largest (overall) dinosaur known
from complete skeleton*

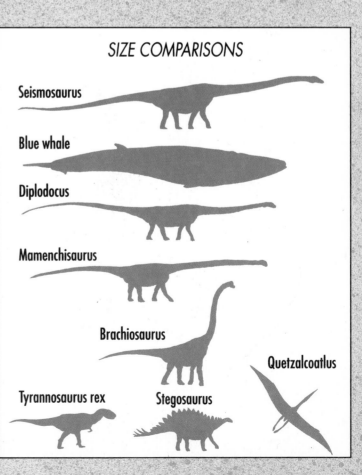

SIZE COMPARISONS

Seismosaurus

Blue whale

Diplodocus

Mamenchisaurus

Brachiosaurus

Quetzalcoatlus

Tyrannosaurus rex   Stegosaurus

THE TALLEST ANIMALS THAT EVER LIVED

THE LONG-NECKED SAUROPODS

THE TALLEST ANIMAL in the world today is the giraffe. One hundred fifty million years ago, it would have been dwarfed by the towering, long-necked **sauropod** dinosaurs, standing more than twice as tall. A museum skeleton of Brachiosaurus, one of the tallest sauropods of all, shows that this high-shouldered dinosaur could have looked into a fifth-floor window if it were alive today.

Some sauropods had longer necks than Brachiosaurus. The longest-necked animal known was Mamenchisaurus. One kind had a neck more than twice as long as a giraffe is tall. If a Mamenchisaurus reared up on its hind legs, it might have been able to reach up higher than Brachiosaurus.

Scientists once thought sauropods wallowed in lakes, using their necks to keep their heads above water. But now they know that water pressing on the necks and chests of sauropods would have suffocated them. Sauropods probably lived on land. They lowered their heads to eat ferns and lifted their heads to nibble leafy branches. Mamenchisaurus would have enjoyed the very highest leaves all to itself!

The heart of one of these skyscraper dinosaurs would have had to be immensely powerful to pump blood all the way up to its brain. Some scientists

HIGH BROWSERS

If the tallest creatures the world has ever seen came together, which animal could reach the highest? (Compare it with the human pictured at the bottom.) Indricotherium (*see pages 14-15*), an Asian rhinoceros, was the tallest of the prehistoric mammals. Dinornis ("terrible bird") may have been the tallest bird. It died out in New Zealand about four hundred years ago. Both these large animals, if they had lived in the age of the dinosaurs, would have walked in the shadows of the giant sauropods. Seismosaurus and Brachiosaurus lived in North America; Mamenchisaurus lived in Asia.

BRACHIOSAURUS
46 feet (14 m)
Tallest animal known from a complete skeleton

SEISMOSAURUS
39 feet (12 m)
Longest dinosaur

INDRICOTHERIUM
24 feet (7.3 m)
Tallest-ever mammal

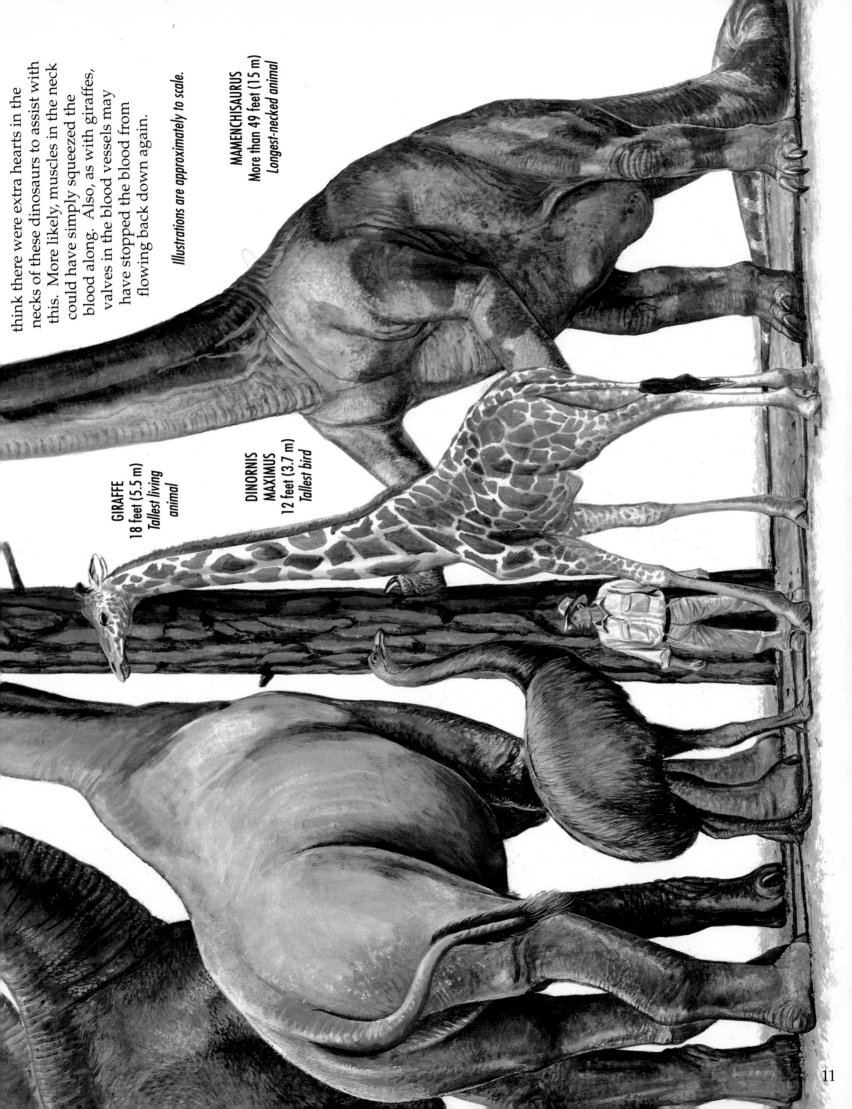

think there were extra hearts in the necks of these dinosaurs to assist with this. More likely, muscles in the neck could have simply squeezed the blood along. Also, as with giraffes, valves in the blood vessels may have stopped the blood from flowing back down again.

Illustrations are approximately to scale.

MAMENCHISAURUS
More than 49 feet (15 m)
Longest-necked animal

GIRAFFE
18 feet (5.5 m)
Tallest living animal

DINORNIS MAXIMUS
12 feet (3.7 m)
Tallest bird

SPRINT CHAMPION

Dromiceiomimus ("emu mimic") *(below)* was a birdlike dinosaur, built similarly to the ostrich. With its long legs, it could have taken very long, fast strides. If it were alive today, this dinosaur might have outrun an ostrich, which sprints at 40 miles (65 km) per hour. Dromiceiomimus lived in southwest Canada 75 million years ago.

Therizinosaurus ("scythe lizard") was named for its huge finger claws *(right)*, shaped like sickle blades. A claw's curved outer edge was 35 inches (90 centimeters) long. Only the arm and hand bones of this dinosaur have been found. Therizinosaurus was as much as 40 feet (12 m) long. It lived in Mongolia 73 million years ago.

Troodon ("wounding tooth") *(below, front)* had a bigger brain for its body size than perhaps any other dinosaur. This agile hunter was as intelligent as birds and even some mammals — the opossum, for example. It lived in the same time and place as Dromiceiomimus.

THE LARGEST SKULL
DINOSAUR RECORD HOLDERS

Horned Torosaurus ("bull lizard") *(below)* had a massive skull. It was about the size of a small car. From its beak to the back of its neck frill, Torosaurus was 8.5 feet (2.6 m) long. This plant-eating dinosaur lived in North America 70 million years ago.

FROM FOSSILS, scientists have determined which dinosaurs were unique in various ways. This illustration shows five types of dinosaurs that hold a record of one kind or another. Torosaurus had the largest head of any animal that ever lived on land. The longest claws belonged to Therizinosaurus. Dromiceiomimus, with its long, thin legs, might have been the fastest-running dinosaur. The smallest dinosaur was, many scientists believe, Compsognathus. Troodon and its relatives were probably the most intelligent of all the dinosaurs.

Illustrations are approximately to scale.

The size of the eight-year-old child *(right)* gives an idea of the sizes of the dinosaurs.

Compsognathus ("elegant jaw") *(left, front)* was a quick hunter. Just 30 inches (75 cm) long, it was not much bigger than a chicken. Compsognathus lived in Europe 150 million years ago.

13

THE LARGEST-EVER LAND MAMMAL
INDRICOTHERIUM, THE GIANT RHINOCEROS

THE FIRST MAMMALS were no bigger than shrews (*see page 7*). Yet, some of their **descendants** were **prehistoric** rhinoceroses, elephants, and other animals that weighed several tons. Being big gave these giant animals advantages. They could eat leafy twigs too high for smaller creatures to reach. In addition, their size and tough hides protected them from the teeth and claws of carnivores — although some of the carnivores, like Andrewsarchus, had grown massive, too.

The largest land mammal the world has ever seen was a giant prehistoric rhinoceros. Called Indricotherium, this mighty animal roamed Asia about 30 million years ago. After studying its fossil bones, scientists at first believed that a living Indricotherium weighed as much as 33 tons (30 metric tons). A closer look showed that Indricotherium normally weighed "only" about 12 tons (11 metric tons), twice as much as an African elephant!

The very largest Indricotherium probably weighed up to 22 tons (20 metric tons). This giant would have been as heavy as ten of today's rhinoceroses. From snout to tail, Indricotherium might have measured up to 36 feet (11 m) — longer than a doubles tennis court is wide. It was so tall that a giraffe's head would only reach up to its shoulders (*see pages 10-11*). Indricotherium was different from the rhinoceros in another way — it had no horns on its head.

This illustration compares an average-size human with giant prehistoric mammals of various kinds.

ANDREWSARCHUS
13 feet (4 m) long
Largest carnivorous mammal

INDRICOTHERIUM
Up to 18 feet (5.5 m)
high at the shoulder
Largest land mammal

MAMMAL GIANTS

Each prehistoric land mammal pictured was the biggest or the heaviest of its kind. Andrewsarchus was the largest-known flesh-eating land mammal. It was similar to a cross between a bear and a hyena. This ferocious animal lived in eastern Asia forty million years ago.

The steppe mammoth, *Mammuthus trogontherii*, was the largest-ever member of the elephant family. Roaming Europe in the depths of the **Ice Ages**, its shaggy coat kept it warm in the bitterly cold winters.

Gigantopithecus, the largest ape, lived in east and southeast Asia, also during Ice Age times. Standing about 10 feet (3 m) tall, it would have been as heavy as a large pony. Early humans might well have met this giant face to face. But Gigantopithecus, a harmless plant-eater, would probably have left humans alone. Some people think Gigantopithecus never became extinct but survives to this day in the Himalayas, where it is known as the Yeti.

Glyptodon was a South American Ice Age mammal related to modern armadillos. Its thick, bony armor probably made this creature the heaviest and best protected mammal of its kind. Glyptodon even had a bony "hat" protecting its head, plus bony rings around its tail.

Illustrations are approximately to scale.

MAMMUTHUS TROGONTHERII
Up to 15 feet (4.5 m)
high at the shoulder
Largest elephant

GIGANTOPITHECUS
Up to 10 feet (3 m) tall
Largest primate

GLYPTODON
Shell 8.2 feet (2.5 m) long
Most heavily armored mammal

15

THE FIRST HUMANS
OUR EARLIEST ANCESTORS

In 1856, miners found an unusual skeleton in a limestone quarry in the Neander Thal (Neander Valley) in Germany. The skull was apelike, and the leg bones were strong and curved. At the time, some scientists thought this Neanderthal person had been a soldier who died in a war about fifty years earlier. Scientists later realized the skeleton belonged to a prehistoric human who died fifty thousand years ago! Since then, even older human bones have been discovered. Most scientists now believe that humans, apes, and monkeys (mammals in the group called primates) all share one ancestor. That ancestor may have been Aegyptopithecus that lived in Egypt 35 million years ago.

Thirteen million years later, the first apelike animals were climbing trees in East Africa. From their descendants came today's chimpanzee and gorilla — and the now-extinct australopithecines. A skeleton of an australopithecine was dug up in Africa in 1974. Called Lucy by the scientists who found her bones, she probably walked upright about five million years ago. She was the first **hominid**, or humanlike animal.

By two million years ago, the first authentic humans, *Homo rudolfensis*, and the closely related *Homo habilis*, appeared. *Homo habilis* could use tools and talk a little. By 200,000 years later, *Homo habilis* had given rise to a bigger, brainier kind of prehistoric human — *Homo erectus*.

Homo sapiens, the first modern human, appeared, scientists believe, about 400,000 years ago. There were once two types of *Homo sapiens* — the Neanderthals, who died out about 30,000 years ago, and humans almost like ourselves.

Aegyptopithecus ("Egyptian ape") *(above)* was the earliest-known primate belonging to Anthropoidea, a group of mammals that includes monkeys, apes, and humans. Weighing about the same as a human baby, Aegyptopithecus climbed on all fours.

Homo rudolfensis (below), the first creature that could be described as "human," lived in Africa about 2.3 million years ago. About the same height as *Australopithecus afarensis,* it had a bigger brain. It made rough stone tools and simple shelters.

THE FIRST TRAVELER

Homo erectus ("upright human") grew to about the same size as a modern human, but it had jutting brows and jaws unlike our own. It was the first fire-user, perhaps the first human hunter of big game, and the first hominid to make the journey from Africa to cooler lands in Asia and Europe. *Homo erectus* lived 1,800,000 to 400,000 years ago.

Neanderthal *(near right)* and a modern human *(far right)* both belonged to the big-brained species, *Homo sapiens* ("wise man"). Neanderthals became extinct — maybe they were driven away from hunting grounds by modern humans.

THE HUMAN BODY
ANATOMICAL RECORD HOLDERS

THE HUMAN BODY is made of billions of tiny building blocks called cells. Different kinds of cells make up the different tissues that build the bones, muscles, and organs (such as the heart, brain, liver, or skin).

Organs that produce chemicals that help our bodies work are known as glands. Sometimes something goes wrong with the chemicals that control how the body grows. The body may grow scarcely at all, or it may become extremely tall or heavy.

The shortest-known adult is a man less than 23 inches (58 cm) high, shorter than a penguin. The tallest man stood about 9 feet (2.7 m) tall, about the height of an Asian elephant. The lightest woman weighed no more than a little dog. The heaviest-known man outweighed a horse.

Three tiny bones are found inside the human ear, attached to the eardrum. These bones are called the hammer, the anvil, and, tiniest of all, the stirrup, or **stapes**. The eardrum vibrates to sounds. Then these three bones pass the vibrations on to the inner ear, which sends signals to the brain.

Inner ear

Eardrum

KEY

1 Tooth enamel *Hardest tissue*
2 Liver *Largest gland* Average weight 3 pounds (1.4 kilograms)
3 Skin *Largest organ* Average size 20 square feet (1.9 sq m)
4 Stapes in middle ear *Smallest bone* 0.12 inches (3 millimeters)
5 Femur (thigh bone) *Largest bone* More than a quarter of total body length
6 Stapedius (moves the stapes) *Smallest muscle*
7 Gluteus maximus (buttock muscle) *Largest muscle*

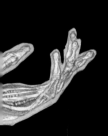

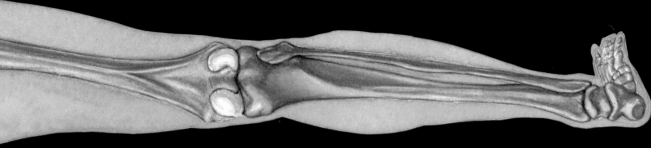

5

GIRAFFE NECKS

The world's longest necks belong to the Padaung women of Myanmar (Burma). A young Padaung girl has a neck of normal length. But soon, brass rings are placed around her neck. Even when the rings fill her entire neck, more are squeezed in, one at a time. This slowly stretches the neck. Some necks grow to at least 15 inches (38 cm) long. A woman with a giraffelike neck seems bizarre in many cultures. But to the Padaung, it is a sign of beauty.

THE TALLEST AND THE SHORTEST

The world's tallest and shortest peoples live in Africa. The Watutsi (Tutsi) of Rwanda and Burundi and the Dinka of Sudan are the tallest. The Bambuti of Zaire are the shortest. The tiny Bambuti need less food than most people to survive.

DINKA (*left*)
Up to 7 feet (2.1 m) tall
One of the world's tallest peoples

BAMBUTI (*right*)
About 4.6 feet (1.4 m) tall
The world's shortest people

THE LARGEST ANIMAL THAT EVER LIVED
THE INCREDIBLE BLUE WHALE

THE BLUE WHALE is probably the biggest creature of all time. The longest recorded specimen was more than 105 feet (32 m), one-third the length of a football field (in this illustration, it would run over six pages). The heaviest ever caught weighed more than 209 tons (190 metric tons). Even an "ordinary" blue whale is as heavy as more than 1,800 people!

Blue whales can grow to this size because water supports their colossal bodies. On dry land, they would collapse under their own weight, even if they had legs instead of flippers. Although blue whales can never leave the sea, they must come up to the surface to breathe air like any other mammal.

The world's largest animal feeds on tiny, shrimplike creatures called krill. One blue whale eats about 4.4 tons (4 metric tons) of krill every day. It swims open-mouthed, trapping krill on the whalebone "comb" that hangs down inside its huge mouth.

While blue whales are the largest baleen whales, sperm whales are the biggest whales that have teeth. A sperm whale is shorter and lighter than a blue whale, with as much as one-third of its length taken up by its enormous head. The sperm whale has two other records to its name — it has the largest brain of any animal, and it is the champion mammalian diver (see pages 34-35).

SPERM WHALE
69 feet (21 m) long
77 tons (70 metric tons)
Largest toothed whale

A BLUE WHALE CALF

A newborn blue whale is as heavy as a large, adult hippopotamus. By the time the whale is a year old, its weight has multiplied eight times.

BLUE WHALE
105 feet (32 m) long
209 tons (190 metric tons)
Largest animal

GIANTS OF THE OCEAN

Illustrations are approximately to scale.

SOUTHERN ELEPHANT SE
22 feet (6.7 m) long
4 tons (3.6 metric tons
Largest seal

GIANT SQUID
57 feet (17.4 m) long
Longest invertebrate

WHALE SHARK
33-49 feet (10-15 m) long
19 tons (17 metric tons)
Largest fish

LEATHERBACK TURTLE
More than 2,117 pounds (960 kg)
*Largest **chelonian***

LITTLE IS KNOWN about whale sharks, the largest fish in the world. They swim, always alone, in tropical waters. Sightings of them are quite rare. The very largest whale sharks can grow to 49 feet (15 m) long and weigh as much as three African elephants. Their broad mouths could engulf two divers at a time but, happily, these are peaceful giants, harmless to humans. Their tiny teeth are only 1/4 inch (6 mm) long. Whale sharks are content to swim along with their mouths open, ready to swallow hundreds of small fish and shrimp. In fact, they travel so slowly that sometimes they collide with boats. Usually, it is the boat that suffers most.

23

LARGEST ON LAND

...AND IN THE AIR

GIRAFFE
18 feet (5.5 m) tall
Tallest land animal

POLAR BEAR
2,205 pounds (1,000 kg)
Largest carnivore on land

KORI BUSTARD
42 pounds (19 kg)
Heaviest flying bird

**ALDABRA GIANT
TORTOISE**
662 pounds (300 kg)
Heaviest land chelonian

AFRICAN ELEPHANTS are the largest land animals in existence today. A newborn African elephant can be twice as heavy as a fully grown man. The heaviest known adult elephant weighed 13 tons (12 metric tons), or as much as twenty-three racehorses! An African elephant may stand 13 feet (4 m) high and grow tusks as long as a small car. It may spend up to twenty hours a day searching for leaves to eat and water to drink. One African elephant can drink enough to fill 550 beverage glasses and eat enough to fill 1,500 cereal bowls in a single day.

Illustrations are approximately to scale.

WANDERING ALBATROSS
12 feet (3.7 m) wingspan
Greatest wingspan

On a scale, a large ostrich would balance a human family made of a man, a woman, and two young children. Besides being the largest bird that exists, the ostrich lays the largest eggs. Each egg is about 8 inches (20 cm) long and as heavy as forty hens' eggs. Sometimes several ostriches lay up to sixty eggs in one nest.

OSTRICH
9 feet (2.7 m) tall
Largest living bird

AFRICAN ELEPHANT
13 tons (12 metric tons)
Largest land animal

ESTUARINE CROCODILE
28 feet (8.5 m) long
Largest reptile

RETICULATED PYTHON
33 feet (10 m)
Longest snake

25

THE SMALLEST ANIMALS
PICTURED AT ACTUAL SIZE

SMALL ANIMALS always live in danger of being gobbled up by larger ones. Yet being small does have its advantages. The fairy fly can lay its tiny eggs on top of the eggs of insects larger than itself. These become food for the fairy fly's grubs when they hatch. A least weasel is slim enough to chase mice down their holes. The tiniest fishes, lizards, mice, and shrews can hide in holes or cracks too narrow for their enemies to enter. The lightweight lesser mouse lemur can climb on twigs that would not bear a monkey's weight. Tiny bats are agile flyers. They dart here and there in pursuit of small moths. Bee-sized hummingbirds can hover in mid-air to drink nectar from flowers.

Some animal-like creatures are so small they are invisible to the eye. They cannot be seen even under a magnifying glass. These mini-creatures are *protozoa*, a name that means "first animals." Most animals are made of millions of tiny building blocks called cells, but a protozoan consists of just a single cell. Some protozoa are so small that thousands could live on your thumbnail. One organism, called a mycoplasma, is the smallest form of life capable of living by itself. It would have to be magnified ten thousand times for it to appear the size of a period on this page!

BEE HUMMINGBIRD
2.1 inches (5.4 cm)
Smallest bird

Even some moths grow larger than a male bee humming-bird *(above)*, the smallest bird. In flight, its tiny whirring wings hum like a bee's. Bee humming-birds live in Cuba and on the nearby Isle of Pines.

This magnifying glass *(right)* reveals three tiny creatures magnified to twice actual size. Dwarf gobies are the lightest of all the backboned animals. Fairy flies (magnified 1,400 times) are wasps small enough to walk through a needle's eye.

DWARF GECKO
0.79 inch (2 cm)
Smallest reptile

BRAZILIAN SHORT-HEADED FROG
0.39 inch (1 cm)
Smallest amphibian

DWARF GOBY
0.32 inch (0.8 cm)
Smallest fish

FAIRY FLY
0.00079 inch (0.02 mm)
Smallest insect

LEAST WEASEL
7.09 inches (18 cm)
Smallest carnivore

Least weasels are the smallest of all meat-eating mammals. Despite their tiny size, these sharp-toothed carnivores are every bit as fierce as tigers. Many females are only half the weight of males, but they also eat mice and voles. Least weasels live in North America and have close relatives in Asia and Europe.

Lesser mouse lemurs *(below)* are so light, it would take four thousand of these tiny primates to weigh as much as one gorilla, the heaviest primate of all.

LESSER MOUSE LEMUR
10.24 inches (26 cm)
Smallest primate

At only 1 inch (2.5 cm) long, Kitti's hog-nosed bat *(below, right)* is even shorter than the pygmy white-toothed shrew (without its tail) *(right)*. A pygmy shrew is about the size of a big bee, but it eats up to four times its own weight in insects every day.

PYGMY WHITE-TOOTHED SHREW
2.36 inches (6 cm)
Smallest mammal

KITTI'S HOG-NOSED BAT
5.9-inch (15-cm) wingspan
Smallest bat

PYGMY MOUSE
2.9 inches (7.3 cm)
Smallest rodent

At 2.9 inches (7.3 cm) long, pygmy mice *(above)* are the smallest rodents. It would take seven thousand of them to match the weight of one capybara, the biggest rodent.

MINIATURE RECORD HOLDERS

Smallest sea mammal: Heaviside's dolphin *(right)*
Weight: 88 pounds (40 kg); Length: 3.9 feet (1.2 m)

Smallest marsupial (pouched mammal):
Kimberley planigale Weight: 0.14 ounces (4 grams); Length: 2.2 inches (5.7 cm)

Smallest breed of horse: Falabella Weight: 88 pounds (40 kg); Shoulder height: 30 inches (76 cm)

Smallest bear: Sun bear Weight: 60 pounds (27 kg); Shoulder height: 27.6 inches (70 cm)

Smallest wild cat: Rusty-spotted cat Weight: 3 pounds (1.4 kg); Length: 19 inches (48 cm)

Smallest hoofed mammal (left):
Lesser mouse deer Weight: 4.4 pounds (2 kg); Shoulder height: 8 inches (20 cm)

The largest living
dragonfly (below)
has a wingspan of
7.5 inches (19 cm).
The largest-ever
dragonfly had a
wingspan more
than three times
that size.

The largest flea, the
beaver flea (right), is still
very tiny. But even small
fleas can jump 13 inches
(33 cm), equivalent to
humans leaping 689 feet
(210 m).

The largest walking
stick (right) is as thick
as a human finger
and longer than
a man's foot.

THE LARGEST INSECTS
PICTURED AT ACTUAL SIZE

THERE ARE MORE TYPES of insects than any other
animal. Insects also come in many different sizes.
Some are bigger than some small mammals, while
some are so tiny it is impossible to see them without a
magnifying glass. The biggest butterfly is a thousand
times larger than the smallest fairy fly.

Most insects are small, partly because of the way
they breathe. Unlike humans, insects do not have lungs
to force air in and out. Instead, air drifts in and out of
their bodies through little tubes in their sides. This
simple breathing system would not let enough fresh
air reach deep inside the body of too large an animal.

An insect lives inside a hard outer skeleton, like a
suit of armor. As the insect grows, this armor splits
open and falls off to allow a bigger suit to grow in its
place. If beetles or butterflies grew as large and plump
as pigeons, their armor would be so heavy they could
not fly. Some prehistoric insects were much bigger
(although no heavier) than the largest insects now
alive. One prehistoric dragonfly even had the wingspan of a crow.

The world's heaviest insects are the goliath beetles from West Africa *(right)*. One large male goliath beetle is as heavy as fifty pygmy shrews, the lightest land mammals *(see page 27)*. Elephant beetles from Central America are larger than goliaths, but weigh less.

The male Queen Alexandra's birdwing butterfly *(below)* is smaller than the female. His bright colors warn birds that he is poisonous.

The world's largest butterfly, the Queen Alexandra's birdwing, is also probably the rarest. Females *(above)* can grow to 11 inches (28 cm) across the wings. They fly at high altitudes.

The largest cockroach *(left)* has a body nearly 4 inches (10 cm) long. Its **antennae** are even longer.

THE FASTEST

IF ALL THE FASTEST ANIMALS got together to run a race, who would win? First, of course, would be birds. Birds can swoop and glide freely through the air in search of their prey, escaping from their enemies, or covering long distances during **migration**.

After birds would be fish. Although difficult to measure, speeds of over 62 miles (100 km) per hour have been recorded for the sailfish. The fastest runner on land is the cheetah, which chases its prey at up to 70 miles (113 km) per hour, although it cannot keep this up for more than a minute or so. Racehorses are also very fast sprinters, but the fastest land animal over distance is the pronghorn. The hare, with its reputation for speed, is, however, easily outsprinted by the fastest human over short distances. Athletes recording times of under ten seconds for a race of 100 m reach peak speeds of around 27 miles (43 km) per hour during the course of their sprint.

Speeds of spiders and insects are very difficult to track. Dragonflies may be the fastest-flying insects (over short bursts), while tropical cockroaches are probably the fastest-moving insects on land.

Illustrations are not drawn to scale.

BLACK MAMBA 12 miles (19 km) per hour
Fastest snake

HUMAN 27 miles (43 km) per hour

BROWN HARE 16 miles (25 km) per hour

KILLER WHALE 34 miles (55 km) per hour
Fastest mammal in water

RACEHORSE 43 miles (69 km) per hour

OSTRICH 40 miles (65 km) per hour
Fastest bird on land

PRONGHORN 42 miles (67 km) per hour
Fastest mammal over distance

SAILFISH 68 miles (109 km) per hour
Fastest fish

GIANT TORTOISE

SLOTH

SNAIL

LONG-LEGGED SUN SPIDER
10 miles (16 km) per hour
Fastest arachnid

COCKROACH 2.9 miles
(4.6 km) per hour
Fastest insect on land

DRAGONFLY 36 miles
(58 km) per hour
Fastest insect

...AND THE SLOWEST

Bringing up the rear are three animals well known for their slowness. The largest living tortoise, the Aldabra giant tortoise of the Seychelles and Mauritius islands, is capable of covering 1,214 feet (370 m) an hour, which is about 20 feet (6 m) a minute. Although the three-toed sloth spends most of its time asleep, it can travel 16 feet (5 m) in a minute. The snail, however, travels no faster than 6 inches (15 cm) in a one-minute "dash."

STOOPING TO CONQUER

The peregrine falcon is the fastest creature on Earth. A bird of prey, it climbs high in the sky, before folding its wings and diving or "stooping" at speeds of up to 217 miles (350 km) per hour to catch other birds in mid-flight. Small birds die from a single blow from its talons. Large birds die when their necks are broken by a stab from its powerful beak.

CHEETAH 70 miles
(113 km) per hour
Fastest mammal

RED-BREASTED MERGANSER
Over 62 miles
(100 km) per hour

PEREGRINE FALCON 217 miles
(350 km) per hour

Ducks and geese are probably the fastest birds in level flight. Species such as the red-breasted merganser, (a sea duck) are powerful flyers.

JEWEL BEETLE
More than 30 years
Longest-lived insect

JAPANESE GIANT SALAMANDER
More than 50 years
Longest-lived amphibian

WANDERING ALBATROSS
More than 70 years
Longest-lived bird

LAKE STURGEON
More than 80 years
Longest-lived fish

HUMAN

KILLER WHALE
About 100 years
Longest-lived
***marine** mammal*

In some countries, the life
expectancy of women
exceeds 80 years. A few
people have even lived
120 years and more.
A man in Lebanon has
reportedly reached
135 years old.

Killer whales travel in family
pods, or groups, ranging from
5 to 50 members. The females,
or cows, are the dominant
animals. The males live to be
about 50, but the cows may live
as long as a century.

THE LONGEST-LIVED ANIMALS
NATURE'S SENIOR CITIZENS

NO ANIMAL lives forever. Accidents, diseases, or enemies kill many of them while they are still young. For instance, only one Atlantic mackerel fish in every 100,000 is likely to survive more than ninety days. But creatures that escape an early end may live long lives. Animals that live protected lives in zoos often survive to greater ages than they would in the wild.

Tiny animals tend to have the shortest lives. A mayfly, for example, once it gets its wings, usually lives no more than a single day. An albatross or an elephant, on the other hand, can survive many years. After an elephant turns 60, however, its teeth begin to wear out. It can no longer chew, so it eventually dies.

In prehistoric times, few human beings lived to even 40 years. Most died young of hunger, injury, or illness. Now, many people survive to 80 and beyond.

Illustrations are not drawn to scale.

ASIAN ELEPHANT
More than 60 years
Longest-lived land mammal
(after humans)

TUATARA

LONGEST-LIVED REPTILES

Tuataras and tortoises live longer than any other land animals. Tuataras (*above*) are lizardlike creatures found only on small islands off New Zealand. In chilly weather, a tuatara breathes just once an hour. Scientists think creatures that lead such slow-motion lives are capable of living 120 years or more.

Several kinds of tortoises normally live more than 100 years. One giant tortoise died in 1918, 152 years after it was collected (by the French explorer Marion de Fresne from the Seychelles). Known as "Marion's tortoise," it was probably an adult when captured and could have been more than 200 years old when it died!

GIANT TORTOISE
More than 100 years
Longest-lived chelonian

33

REALM OF THE DEEP

THE DEEPEST-LIVING OCEAN ANIMALS

Deep in the oceans, beyond the shallow waters that fringe the continents, lie vast undersea plains. Towering mountain ranges rise from them, while great trenches plunge even deeper — the Marianas Trench in the Pacific Ocean reaches a depth of more than 36,000 feet (11,000 m).

Most marine animal life is found in sunlit shallow waters, down to about 328 feet (100 m). But there are some animals that live at greater depths, eating the remains of animals and plants that have fallen from the surface. And other animals feed on these animals, some diving thousands of feet in search of prey.

Sperm whales are the champion divers. Some males are known to dive to about 9,845 feet (3,000 m) to prey on giant squid. Although they are mammals and need to breathe air, they can stay under water for more than an hour. They dive from and rise to the same point on the surface at great speeds.

Fish and other types of animals live at still greater depths. Brotulid fish frequent deep ocean trenches. They are the deepest-living **vertebrates**. The deepest-living creature of all is the amphipod, a kind of crustacean, that has been found in the Marianas Trench at depths of more than 32,810 feet (10,000 m).

Illustrations are not drawn to scale.

34

Deep in the ocean, in total darkness, live small fish with gaping mouths. Some eat dead animals and plants that have fallen from above. Others give off light to attract live fish, squid, and crustaceans before devouring them.

The measuring rod is marked at 3,281-feet (1,000-m) intervals.

AMPHIPOD
34,450 feet (10,500 m)
Deepest-living invertebrate

Bottom-dwelling animals (right) live off animal and plant remains and living small fish.

KEY

1 Wandering albatross
2 Emperor penguin *Deepest-diving bird* 870 feet (265 m)
3 Human *Deepest dive* about 1,640 feet (500 m)
4 Leatherback turtle *Deepest-diving reptile* 3,937 feet (1,200 m)
5 Elephant seal *Deepest-diving seal* 4,100 feet (1,250 m)
6 Bathysphere *Record descent* 3,028 feet (923 m)
7 Giant squid
8 Sixgill shark
9 *Alvin* submersible
10 Sperm whale *Deepest-diving mammal* over 9,843 feet (3,000 m)
11 Anglerfish
12 Gulper
13 Wreck of *Titanic* about 13,125 feet (4,000 m)
14 Vampire squid
15 Rat-tail fish
16 Hatchet fish
17 Anglerfish
18 Tripod fish
19 Sponge *Deepest-living* 18,046 feet (5,500 m)
20 Brotulid *Deepest-living fish* 27,232 feet (8,300 m)
21 Starfish *Deepest-living* 24,608 feet (7,500 m)
22 *Trieste* bathyscaphe *Record descent* 35,842 feet (10,924 m)

OCEAN TRAVELERS
THE LONGEST JOURNEYS

ANIMALS ARE ALWAYS ON THE MOVE in search of food. Some travel at the same time each year to places where a new season brings a better climate for feeding or **breeding**. Called migration, these journeys are sometimes made to distant parts of the world. Each year, ambitious travelers fly or swim incredible distances across oceans and back to the same places.

The champion long-distance specialist is the Arctic tern. In one year, this small bird flies from the Arctic to the Antarctic and back again — almost all the way around the world. The wandering albatross also circles the world, but near the South Pole where the distance is shorter.

Animal swimmers can also make amazingly long sea trips. Green turtles feed off Brazil but swim far out into the Atlantic Ocean to breed on Ascension Island. Gray whales make the longest journeys of any mammal. They feed in Arctic waters in summer before swimming south in winter to breed off Mexico.

European eel

Arctic tern

A T L A N T I C

O C E A N

Green turtle

The young of the European eel *(right)* are born in the Sargasso Sea east of Florida. They spend the next few years drifting over 6,200 miles (10,000 km) to Europe. They swim up rivers and grow into adults.

The wandering albatross *(below)* travels around the world near Antarctica.

The albacore *(bottom)* may make two journeys across the Pacific totaling 9,820 miles (15,800 km).

Probably the farthest-traveled reptile, the green turtle *(above)* swims nearly 1,400 miles (2,250 km) to its breeding grounds on Ascension Island and back again.

Illustrations are not drawn to scale.

A BIRD OF TWO SUMMERS

All terns migrate, but none as far as the Arctic tern *(left)*. Adults breed in the Arctic when it is summer in the north. Then they fly to the opposite end of Earth, a distance of about 8,100 miles (13,000 km), where they spend the southern summer eating the fish off Antarctica. For half a year, they live where the sun never sets. Their migrations are so long that Arctic terns spend the other half of the year just flying from one home to another. Over the course of their lives, some terns fly more than 621,400 miles (1 million km).

The slender-billed shearwater *(left)* nests on islands near Australia and then goes on a seven-month journey around the north Pacific. It makes use of winds to help it complete its figure-eight marathon.

Pacific salmon *(below)* travel out to sea and back to their "home" rivers, a journey of over 7,020 miles (11,300 km).

No other mammal migrates as far as the gray whale *(below)*. In one year, it may swim 14,000 miles (22,500 km).

Pacific salmon

Albacore

Gray whale

PACIFIC

OCEAN

Slender-billed shearwater

Wandering albatross

OVERLAND TRAVELERS
LONG-DISTANCE SPECIALISTS

MANY ANIMAL MIGRANTS that travel by air — birds, bats, and insects — prefer to avoid flying over long stretches of water. The water might prevent them from finding their usual sources of food or from resting after long periods of flight. If they do need to cross large bodies of water on their journey, they will cross where there are narrow straits or island "stepping-stones."

In spring in the Northern Hemisphere, millions of birds flock thousands of miles northward. Warblers, plovers, and others rear their young during the long northern summer days when food is plentiful. Bats and butterflies join in the great airborne migration. In addition, herds of caribou wander on foot hundreds of miles across the far north of Canada.

Sometimes, the travelers must cross deserts. These are just as forbidding as the open seas. Warblers eat heartily before they fly over a desert. A plump willow warbler's body holds enough energy to enable it to fly sixty hours nonstop.

As summer ends, the long-distance travelers, or their young, head south to spend winter in warmer climates.

Probably the farthest-traveled bat, the noctule (above) flies up to 1,000 miles (1,600 km) north across eastern Europe in the spring.

Golden plovers (above) fly over land from Brazil to northern Canada, then back across the Atlantic Ocean. This is a flight of about 11,800 miles (19,000 km) each year.

Every fall, clouds of monarch butterflies (right) flutter almost 2,000 miles (3,200 km) south from Canada to Mexico. Billions of these insects spend winter clustered together on tall evergreen trees. In spring, they fly back north, laying eggs as they go. Most adults die, but their young complete the journey begun by their parents.

Caribou

NORTH AMERICA

Monarch butterfly

Golden plover

SO
AMEI

The willow warbler *(left)* may undergo a journey from northern Siberia to the southern tip of Africa — farther than any other perching bird.

Willow warbler

Noctule bat

Painted lady

EUROPE

ASIA

Desert locust

AFRICA

Illustrations are not drawn to scale.

Painted ladies *(left)* are the farthest-traveled **Old World** butterflies.

Huge swarms of desert locusts *(below)* will fly almost 2,000 miles (3,200 km) in a great circle around the Sahara Desert. They probably fly farther than any other insect, except the butterfly.

ARCTIC OVERLANDERS

Named after the American Indian word for "shoveler," caribou *(left)* paw away snow to eat the grass underneath. The caribou walks farther in a year than any other mammal. Each spring, herds trudge over 800 miles (1,300 km) along well-worn tracks to their summer pastures north of the Arctic Circle in Canada. In the treeless lands, the melting snows uncover fresh new grasses and other tasty plants. Caribou fatten up in preparation for the long return journey to their winter home in the deep **coniferous** forests of Alberta, Saskatchewan, and Manitoba.

THE RAREST ANIMALS
CREATURES CLOSEST TO EXTINCTION

SOME ANIMALS ARE VERY RARE, numbering perhaps only a few hundred in the wild. They include some very well-known animals, like the giant panda or the blue whale. These animals are **endangered**. They are becoming very scarce and could soon disappear forever.

In the course of evolution *(see page 7)*, every kind of animal eventually dies out, but humans are speeding up the rate at which many animal **species** become extinct. In the past, hunters were the worst culprits, killing animals for food or sport. But now, most wild creatures die out because of loss of **habitat** — farms and cities gobble up the forests, prairies, and marshes where the animals live.

In 1990, scientists counted about 5,000 kinds of animals known to be at risk of extinction — 2,000 invertebrates, more than 1,000 birds, about 760 fishes, about 700 mammals, nearly 200 reptiles, and 63 amphibians (frogs, toads, and salamanders). Besides all these, millions of unknown kinds of insects could vanish forever even before they have been discovered!

Fewer than three hundred Tonkin snub-nosed monkeys *(right)* live in the wild, in four small patches of bamboo forest in Vietnam.

By 1990, only one Spix's macaw *(below)* remained in the wild in Brazil. Thirty more were kept as pets. Breeding these birds in captivity seems the only hope of keeping this species alive.

The Javan rhinoceros *(above)* is the scarcest large mammal. A century ago, thousands roamed the hilly forests of southeast Asia. Then farmers destroyed the habitat, and hunters killed the rhinoceroses to sell the horns. Only about seventy rhinos survive.

The vaquita *(right)* lives only in the Gulf of California. It dies in nets set for sharks and rays. Only two hundred of these tiny whales, each no longer than a human, still survive.

Illustrations are not drawn to scale.

A SUCCESS STORY?

Of the animals pictured here, only the black-footed ferret *(below)*, which is enjoying the special care of people determined to save it, has a good chance of survival. In the mid-1980s, there were just a dozen of these ferrets left, all in Wyoming. Scientists caught and bred them. By 1991, their numbers had risen to 325.

Kemp's ridley sea turtle *(below)* breeds mainly on one beach in Mexico. Once, tens of thousands made their way to the beach. Now only a few hundred arrive. Many drown in fishing nets or die in oil-polluted waters.

PRECARIOUS POND DWELLERS

Changes in the weather can put some animals at risk. Golden toads lived only in Costa Rica's moist, misty mountain forests. In 1988, little rain fell and the toads' breeding ponds dried up. By 1990, no toads could be found at all.

The Devil's Hole pupfish lives only in a flooded Californian cave. If the pool dries up, the little fish could disappear forever.

THE TALLEST TREES
NATURE'S SKYSCRAPERS

TREES CAN GROW much higher and heavier than any other living thing. The tallest known tree was a Douglas Fir — it was felled on Vancouver Island, British Columbia one hundred years ago. It was 420 feet (128 m) tall. The tallest trees that exist today are the coast redwoods in northern California.

The heaviest living tree and the most massive living thing of all is another kind of redwood from California. Called "General Sherman," this giant sequoia, perhaps more than three thousand years old, is thirteen times heavier than a blue whale, the largest animal. Its trunk is 82 feet (25 m) wide just above the ground. You can punch its thick, spongy bark without hurting your hand!

Trees can live longer than almost any other kind of plant. The world's oldest tree is a bristlecone pine growing high on a mountain in Nevada. More than five thousand years old, it would have begun life around the same time as the dawn of the ancient Egyptian civilization. Probably the oldest kind of living tree is the maidenhair, or ginkgo. Its fan-shaped leaves look almost exactly like fossil leaves preserved in rocks known to be more than 160 million years old.

GIANT SEQUOIA
2,755 tons (2,500 metric tons)
Heaviest living tree

EUCALYPTUS (MOUNTAIN ASH)
348 feet (106 m) tall
Tallest broadleaf tree

COAST REDWOOD
367 feet (112 m) tall
Tallest living tree

DOUGLAS FIR
420 feet (128 m) tall
Tallest known tree

42

The banyan tree (below, background), a kind of fig, is a holy tree in India. Its roots grow downward from its branches and support them like pillars. This allows these trees to keep growing outward.

A fat baobab tree (below) can measure more than 164 feet (50 m) around its trunk. Its huge, bottle-shaped trunk is for storing water during the dry season in Africa. In long droughts, some baobabs may shrink in size.

BANYAN TREE
(below, background)
1,970 feet
(600 m) around
*Greatest canopy
(spread of branches)*

The oldest single living tree is a bristlecone pine (below). Bristlecones grow very slowly on the high, windswept slopes of the Rocky Mountains.

The ginkgo (below) is a living fossil, probably the oldest kind of tree alive today. Ginkgoes also existed in the age of the dinosaurs.

GIRAFFE
18 feet (5.5 m)
Tallest animal

Illustrations are approximately to scale.

43

THE LARGEST FLOWER
THE MYSTERIOUS RAFFLESIA

WALKING THROUGH a southeast Asian forest, you might notice a disgusting odor, like rotting meat. This stench would lead you to one of the strangest plants on Earth. A scientist named it *Rafflesia* after Sir Thomas Stamford Raffles, the British colonial governor who founded Singapore. People also call the flower "the stinking corpse lily." But Rafflesia is not a lily, nor is it like any other ordinary flowering plant.

It has no stem, and there are no leaves or roots. The whole plant consists of long, thin threads hidden from sight — and one huge flower up to 3 feet (90 cm) across — the largest flower in the world. With five reddish "petals," resembling slices of raw meat, the flower is very heavy, too. A large specimen may weigh more than a one-year-old child.

THE SMALLEST FLOWER

The picture *(below)* shows Wolffia, the world's tiniest flowering plant, hugely magnified and cut open from the side. Its flowers grow inside a special hollow. About the size of a comma in this paragraph, the Wolffia plant is so small that it cannot be studied without a magnifying glass. Millions of these floating plants mass together to form green scum on ponds. There are several kinds of Wolffia in different parts of the world. The smallest kind, *Wolffia arrhiza*, can be found in Australia.

Rafflesia has a flower almost as big as the wheel of a bus, but no roots, stem, or leaves. It is a **parasite** that steals nourishment from other plants.

Threads that form a new Rafflesia plant sprout from sticky seeds produced by the female flowers. The threads burrow through the rough bark of a jungle vine. Nine months later, a new flower bud bursts open.

THE OLDEST FLOWER

Nobody knows when the world's first flowering plant bloomed, or what type it was. But fossil leaves and pollen found in rocks show that flowering plants existed more than 125 million years ago. The earliest kinds *(left)* may have looked like today's magnolias. Scientists believe the magnolias' ancestors were related to non-flowering, cone-bearing pines and fir trees. Unlike these kinds of plants, flowering plants carry seeds covered with a special outer coat. These well-protected seeds helped flowering plants multiply and spread around the world.

GLOSSARY

amphibians — cold-blooded animals, such as frogs and toads, that live both in water and on land.

ancestor — a being from which another being is born.

antennae — a pair of thin organs on the head of an insect or other animal.

breeding — the reproduction processes of a plant or animal.

chelonian — the family of animals that includes tortoises, turtles, and terrapins.

coniferous — a tree that bears its seeds in cones.

descendants — offspring of a living or once living being.

endangered — the state of being threatened with extinction.

evolution — the slow, gradual development of a species over a vast amount of time.

extinct — no longer in existence.

fossils — the traces of plants or animals from earlier times preserved in rock or Earth's crust.

habitat — a place in nature where animals and plants grow and live.

hominid — any beings in the family of two-footed primate mammals comprising recent humans and their immediate ancestors.

Ice Ages — periods of time in the history of Earth when there was widespread glaciation.

invertebrates — animals that do not have a backbone.

mammals — warm-blooded animals that give birth to live young and that have hair or fur on their bodies. The babies are nourished with the mother's milk.

marine — relating to the sea.

migration — a mass movement of beings from one region to another.

Old World — the Eastern Hemisphere, mainly Europe.

parasite — a plant or animal that lives off a different type of plant or animal in order to survive.

prehistoric — belonging to the time before history was recorded, or written down.

pterosaur — an extinct flying reptile.

reptiles — animals, such as snakes, turtles, and lizards, that crawl on the ground and are cold-blooded.

sauropod — an order of herbivorous dinosaurs that had long necks and tails, small heads, and five-toed limbs.

species — a grouping of animals or plants with similar characteristics.

stapes — the tiniest of the bones found in the ear. The bones of the ear pass sound vibrations on to the inner ear, which sends signals to the brain.

vertebrates — animals that have a backbone.

RESEARCH PROJECTS

1. Visit a sea park or aquarium that is nearest your home. Make a chart on graph paper of the animals you observe there, showing the depths where the marine animals live in the wild. Also, chart the depths to which each of the animals dives in the wild.

2. Visit a zoo or a sea park that is nearest your home. Make a list of the largest animal there; the smallest; and the fastest on land, in the water, and in the air.

3. Trace your family roots by talking to relatives or referring to any written records that may exist. Which of your relatives lived the longest? Is one side of the family more long-lived than the other?

4. Do some research on the animals that can be seen in the area in which you live. Which of them are year-round residents? Which of them migrate? Where do they migrate, and when?

BOOKS

Album of Whales. McGowen (Macmillan)

Bloodthirsty Plants (series). Gentle (Gareth Stevens)

Colors of the Sea (series). Ethan and Bearanger
   (Gareth Stevens)

Endangered! (series). Burton (Gareth Stevens)

The Extinct Species Collection (series). (Gareth Stevens)

Flowers. Jennings (Childrens)

Guinness Book of Records. (Facts on File)

In Peril (series). Behm/Balouet (Gareth Stevens)

Insects Do the Strangest Things. Hornblow (Random)

Lost Forever (series). Behm and Balouet
   (Gareth Stevens)

*Meet the Great Ones: An Introduction to Whales and Other
   Cetaceans.* Barstow (Cetacean Society)

The New Creepy Crawly Collection (series).
   (Gareth Stevens)

The New Dinosaur Collection (series). (Gareth Stevens)

Plants and Flowers. Holley (Penworthy)

Rainbow Encyclopedia of Prehistoric Life. Lambert
   (Macmillan)

Secrets of the Animal World (series). (Gareth Stevens)

Under the Microscope (series). (Gareth Stevens)

The World Almanac. (World Almanac Books)

The World Almanac for Kids. (World Almanac Books)

VIDEOS

Dinosaurs. (Ambrose Video)

Endangered Animals: Will They Survive?
   (Encyclopædia Britannica Educational Corporation)

Flowers. (Multimedia)

The Great Dinosaur Series. (Spoken Arts)

National Geographic: The Great Whales.
   (Columbia Tristar)

NOVA: Animal Olympians. (Image Entertainment)

Prehistoric Humans. (BFA Films)

WEB SITES

www.bodnarchuk.com/prehistoric/dinosaur.html

www.earthwatch.org/ed/home.html

www.worldwildlife.orglaction

www.ex.ac.uk/%7Egjlramel/six.html

www.fws.gov/~r9endspp/endspp.html

rs6000.bvis.uic.edu:80/museum

PLACES TO VISIT

John G. Shedd Aquarium
   1200 South Lake Shore Drive
   Chicago, IL 60605

San Diego Zoo
   2920 Zoo Drive
   San Diego, CA 92103

Vancouver Aquarium in Stanley Park
   Vancouver, British Columbia V6B 3X8

Otto Orkin Insect Zoo
   National Museum of Natural History
   Smithsonian Institution
   10 Constitution Avenue
   Washington, D.C. 20560

Metro Toronto Zoo
   Meadowvale Road
   West Hill, ON M1B 5K7

INDEX